VICTORIAN
NORTHERN CALIFORNIA

SAN FRANCISCO

Few cities have the immediate association with Victorian architecture that San Francisco brings to mind. This is not only due to its large number of Victorian houses, but also because in this densely packed urban setting, these houses sitting on the hills impart a distinctly human element to the environment, proclaiming, "People live here".

In the 1960s, a revolution dubbed *The Colorist Movement* took hold in San Francisco. The resulting *Painted Ladies* have been superbly documented by the far-seeing team of Pomada and Larsen, among others. Today in San Francisco one encounters some of the most creatively painted Victorians in the world. The results are inspiring. These houses uplift the spirit.

The earthquake of 1906 lasted 48 seconds and would have been an 8.5 on the Richter scale. The fire that resulted destroyed downtown San Francisco. Most of the rebuilding in that old area was constructed in later, more subdued styles. The pictures in this volume are located around Alamo Square, Alta Plaza, and Pacific Heights.

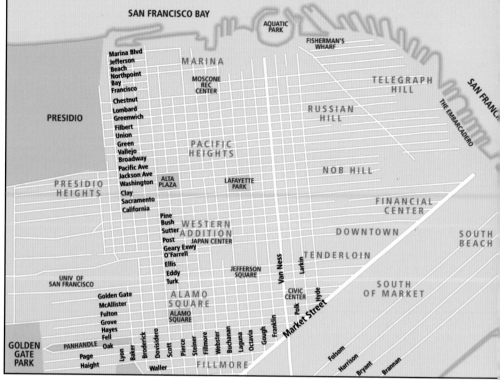

OPPOSITE TOP LEFT: 1347 McAllister between Steiner and Pierce. This French neo-Baroque hybrid was designed with a ballroom on the top floor by architects Dunn & Schroepfer and was built in 1900. The entrance with its elegant curves has been painstakingly restored.

OPPOSITE TOP RIGHT: 1801 Laguna at the corner of Bush. The elaborate roof cornice and stick decorations have been picked out to contrast with the basic blue used for the house. Yet, the overall effect is calm.

OPPOSITE BOTTOM: 1447 McAllister between Pierce and Scott. Stick/Eastlake style. Built in 1889, this is one of a pair of twin homes which sit next to each other. The somber color scheme seems to emphasize rather than obscure the dynamic rhythms of the stick work. The gilded details add just the right touch of splendor.

ABOVE: 700 block of Steiner between Hayes and Grove, facing Alamo Square. Queen Anne style. Called *Postcard Row* because they are so often photographed. While maintaining an overall stylistic unity, these homes are lovingly individualized with detailing.

RIGHT: 2026 California between Octavia and Laguna. Italianate. Built in 1878. After the 1906 earthquake, the owners added the then-fashionable curved glass bay windows. It is quite a hike from the street level just to the front door. Notable is the pharaonic head over the portico, a whimsical touch of ironic seriousness.

2733 California between Scott and Divisidero. Built 1886. The style is Stick/Eastlake. The flowers are incised on the porch columns. The detailing on the porch alone makes for a fantastic house.

2007 Franklin at the corner of Washington.
The Haas-Lilienthal House. Queen Anne.
The grandest Victorian of Pacific Heights
serves as headquarters for the Foundation
for San Francisco's Architectural Heritage.
The house is furnished and can be toured.

UKIAH

Located in Mendocino County, of which it is the county seat, Ukiah is on the banks of the Russian River near Clear Lake and the Pacific Ocean. In 1856, Ukiah's first settler, Samuel Lowry, built a log cabin on the southwest corner of Perkins and Main streets. Ukiah was part of the Yokayo Land Grant. The word Yokayo comes from the Indian word meaning "deep valley".

In 1889 the first train steamed into Ukiah. Land prices quickly boomed with bare lots going from $30.00 to $150.00. The town grew and prospered. Soon drug stores, several saloons, doctor and lawyer offices, and livery and feed stables were built around the courthouse.

The Held-Poage Memorial Home and Research Library, located here in Ukiah, is a treasure trove of historical information on all of Mendocino County.

BELOW: 612 West Smith. Queen Anne style. Built in 1877 by the Reeves family, the house underwent renovations in 1809, 1923, 1947, and 1959. The result is a greatly subdued house compared to the highly decorated gingerbread confection it originally was. In the last renovation both the tower and much of the gingerbread were removed. Nevertheless, what one sees today is a stately structure with a gracious Victorian entrance, generous bay windows on both floors, and enough gingerbread still in place to keep the Victorian spirit well-defined.

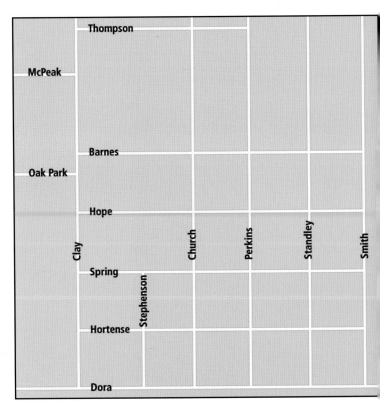

ABOVE: 603 West Perkins at the corner of Dora. **The Held-Poage House.** Queen Anne style with Colonial Revival influence. The architects: Orr and Evans. It was built in 1903 for the then-princely sum of $2,000. It is largely the same now as it was when it was built, with only the addition of a new kitchen and a second bathroom. It is listed on the National Register of Historical Places. This home is now the Held-Poage Research Library and headquarters for the Mendocino County Historical Society.

RIGHT: 204 North Spring. **James R. and Josie Mathews House.** Queen Anne. Built in 1895. Builder: W.C. Lyons. This house was built from published architectural drawings which were very popular in this period. This is a classic Queen Anne cottage. The detailing is carried through in every instance, even the roofing pattern which is continued on the small back building. The gingerbread is restrained and logical.

ABOVE: 214 South Hortense. **The John C. Johnson House.** Neo-Classic, Romanesque Revival. It was built in 1901. With its highly complex shape, multiple and variously shaped dormers, it shares much in common with a grand Queen Anne house. Of particular interest is its wrap-around porch and the way the porch's roof blends harmoniously into the roof of the house itself. The restrained and formal landscaping at the base of the house provides an almost architectural embellishment. The original owner employed one of his ranch hands who was noted for his green thumb to create lovely flower gardens on the property.

LEFT: 616 West Church. **The I.W. and Laura Grover House.** Neo-Classic Revival. It was built in 1906. The Govers built this home so they could be near their recently married only daughter. Local styles influence local styles. It is interesting that this house, the Johnson house, and the Held-Poage house all have circular or multi-sided corner porches. Clearly, this was a status symbol in the area, denoting perhaps the ability and desire to enjoy leisure time.

In 1855, brothers Sam and Harry Baechtel, looking for grazing land, brought cattle from Marin County. Here in this valley they found what they needed and became the first non-native settlers here. Sam Baechtel wrote in his journal that there were about 300 Native Americans who shared the valley. From his reports it seems they got on quite well.

The first grist mill was constructed in 1860 by Williams Janes. Soon the Blosser brothers raised a water-powered sawmill on Willits Creek. The community of Little Lake grew around Baechtel land with a store, meeting house, blacksmith, and saloon. The store built in 1865 by Kirk Brier on Hiram Willits' land became the center of Willitsville. The town incorporated in 1888 and called itself Willits. The population at that time consisted of 720 inhabitants.

The chief factors in the local economy were, as today, lumbering and farming. The Northwestern Railroad reached Willits in 1901, and ten years later came the "Skunk" trains. As Northwestern completed its line from San Francisco to Eureka in 1914, Willits became the center of the line.

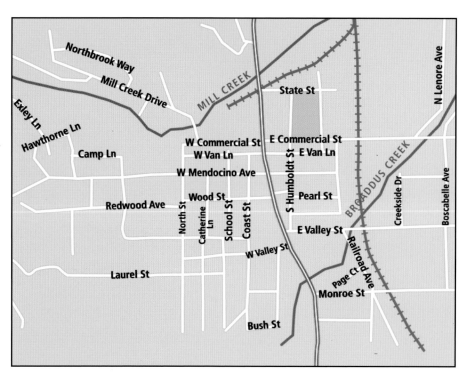

118 School Street. **The A.J. Clay House.** Built around 1900. Queen Anne cottage. This is a snug, moderate size home with large scale ideas about decoration—here wonderfully preserved and painted in cheerful colors. Victorians loved gardens and flowers. This mature garden softens the house in summertime, making it appear smaller than it actually is. This typical Queen Anne cottage is much roomier inside than one might estimate from its exterior.

ABOVE: 166 School Street. **The Willits House.** Built circa 1901. Queen Anne cottage. Groups of houses in a given locale form an idiom which is copied over and over with variations. This leads to a local or vernacular style. This house and the one down the block from it at 118 School Street (shown on page 11) have just such a relationship. Built a year apart, with slightly different aims perhaps, but still remarkably similar.

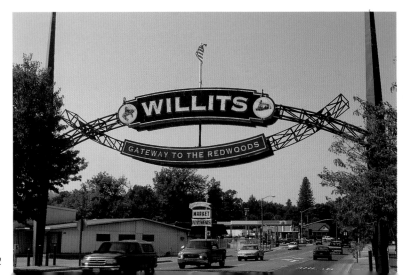

OPPOSITE TOP: 84 State Street at the corner of South Humboldt. **The L.J. Roach House.** Queen Anne style. Built in 1904. Here just 15 miles north of Ukiah and built in the same time frame, it is interesting to see a similarly emphasized treatment of the porch and roof. (Compare with the Held-Poage, the Johnson, and the Grover houses.) The whimsical and well-proportioned witch's hat tower together with the rhythmic bric-a-brac set off this otherwise somber house very well. Victorians wanted to display social status in a way that was not overly formal. This house clearly proclaims its social superiority. Sitting on this porch, one would look out onto a large, tree-filled park, an added bonus.

OPPOSITE BOTTOM: 182 East Valley Street. **The Presley McPeak House.** Built 1905. Queen Anne cottage. With this quiet color scheme, the jaunty porch trusses and lively picket fence, this little Victorian is a picture of the good life dreamed of and indeed enjoyed by prosperous middle-class Americans at the turn of the century. The willow tree in the front yard clearly has been a steady companion for the house over many decades.

Mendocino was listed as a post office in 1858. The native Pomo Indians had their villages near the mouth of the Big River. The first white settler, William Kasten, is said to have been the lone survivor of a small boat wrecked off the Mendocino coast in 1850. Reports to San Francisco-based lumber concerns regarding this area's great redwood forests led to the building of a mill at Big River in 1852. By 1865 the population had grown to 700. Until about 1870 most of the buildings were along Main and west of Kasten Street.

Most of the houses and commercial buildings in Mendocino, which are from the second half of the 19th century, were designed by New Englanders. Next to the Victorian San Francisco style, the New England taste reflected here, although not without Victorian embellishment, is comparatively subdued. Mendocino has a very attractive setting, lying on a small peninsula thrusting into Mendocino Bay. Historical awareness in Mendocino it has been cultivated to a high degree.

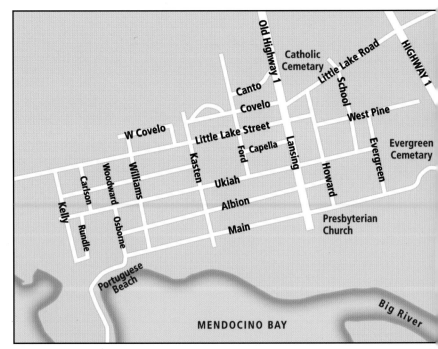

Albion Street. **The MacCallum House.** Built 1881. Queen Anne. One of the most outstanding houses in a town with several outstanding examples of Victorian architecture. MacCallum had married two years before the house was built, and he and his wife lived with her parents until the new home was ready. In 1908, after MacCallum died, his wife had the house moved to its present location. It had been closer to Ukiah and farther west. MacCallum chose a symmetrical layout for his house, whereas the typical Queen Anne house is asymmetrical. Strip away the glassed-in section of the porch and the complete symmetry is revealed. The large scale gingerbread on this house is also unusual. The decorative boards attached to the dormers under the gable roof are repeated on the other two large dormers with which they intersect. Today this beautiful and imposing house is an inn and restaurant.

TOP: Little Lake Street. **The Spencer Hills House.** Built 1855, then the site of a 250 acre cattle ranch. One of Mendocino's oldest and most beautiful homes. The ell and the porch were added later. It has large windows and a particularly beautiful bargeboard attached to the eaves.

ABOVE: Corner of Kasten and Capella. **The Denslow-Maxwell House.** Queen Anne. Built 1879. Representing a very different point of view from the MacCallum house, architecturally speaking, a turreted Victorian unlike any other in Mendocino. In fact, the placement of this turret would be unusual anywhere. Unusual or not, it is true to the Victorian love of surprise in architecture. It is certainly an elegant house. And guess what? The house is reported to have a ghost!

TOP: Little Lake Street. **The Albert Brown House.** Built by Sophie Cranz in 1879. Queen Anne. Albert Brown and his wife had lived in the house for a long time before they died in old age—long enough to have the house named for him. Brown started the first electric company in Mendocino. Various owners have changed much about the house but the front facade remains pretty much as it was when built. The matching bay windows (again Mendocino symmetry) would give the dwellers a good view of village life.

RIGHT: Main Street. **The Mendocino Hotel.** The false front once joined two buildings, the second being built in 1878. It was run as *The Central Hotel* by the Bever brothers for 25 years. In 1975 the hotel was bought and restored by Mendocino-born R.O. Peterson and rebuilt behind the historic facade. The balcony is both entertaining for guests and protection from rain for pedestrians.

ABOVE: Main Street. **The McCornack House.** Dr. William McCornack built it in 1882. Queen Anne. McCornack left Mendocino in 1887 to open a hospital in Fort Bragg, but subsequent owners were also doctors and, as a result, the house is known as "The House of the Doctors". Today it is the Mendocino Village Inn. The gambrel roof is a noteworthy feature here as are the framed dormer windows. Victorian designers chose roof designs from both the practical side (gambrel roofing makes the interior space feel and look larger) and the aesthetic. To the right of the house is a water tower which most houses in Mendocino had originally. Most of these water towers have been lost to age or demolition.

LEFT: Little Lake Street. **The Maxwell-Jarvis House.** Italianate. Built in 1878 by Albert Maxwell, a contractor who had built the Presbyterian Church and several other important Mendocino structures. Maxwell and his wife had come from Maine where, as in the Northeast generally, the Italianate style was well-established and popular. Note the quoins at the corners of the house, a typical Italianate detail. Very elaborate Italianate homes were often crowned by a cupola. Here, a double dormer does the trick.

FORT BRAGG

I n 1857, a military post was established on the Mendocino Indian Reservation and named for Captain Braxton Bragg. By 1867, the reservation and military outpost at Fort Bragg were abandoned. Small lumber mills were being built by 1869 at the mouth of every creek. Ranches were settled. By 1873, Fort Bragg had an established lumber port at Noyo. The Fort Bragg Railroad was founded to haul logs to the mill. A San Francisco streetcar was purchased to carry loggers and their families on Sunday excursions to the woods. Fort Bragg was incorporated in 1889.

At the turn of the century, the only link to manufactured creature comforts and staples like sugar and coffee were from delivery by steamship. In 1905, the California Western Railroad and Navigation Company was formed. Plans were pushed to get the rail line all the way to Willits where train connections could be made for San Francisco. The 1906 earthquake resulted in a fire that threatened the entire city. Within the town itself, all brick buildings were damaged, if not destroyed completely, and many frame homes were knocked off their piers. The fire downtown burned the entire block bordered by Franklin, Redwood and McPherson Streets, plus the west side of Franklin. The West Franklin block burned down to approximately one half block beyond the intersection of Redwood and Franklin.

Within 12 months following the earthquake, all downtown reconstruction was completed. Ironically, the earthquake brought real prosperity to Fort Bragg as its mills furnished lumber to rebuild San Francisco. With the new prosperity, the rail line to Willits was completed, and in 1912 the first tourists came to Fort Bragg. By 1916 Fort Bragg had become a popular place to visit—and to settle.

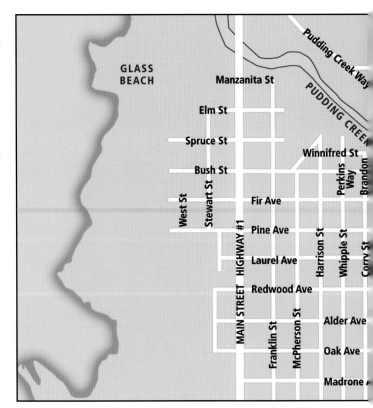

632 North Main Street. Now the Country Inn Bed & Breakfast. Queen Anne. The earliest existing records show that this house was purchased by L.A. Moody from the Union Lumber Company for $500. The pyramid roof is typical of early Fort Bragg residences. The gingerbread was added sometime in the 1970s.

Guest House Museum. North Main Street between Redwood and Laurel. Queen Anne. Built 1892 by T.L. Johnson on the site of the military post hospital. This is a large and rather austere looking building enlivened by a dramatic roofline and a robust overall geometry. In 1979 Georgia-Pacific undertook a restoration of the building. The Guest House Museum is the repository of artifacts and records telling the story of Fort Bragg. This large house sits on a promontory between Main Street and the ocean.

TOP: North Main Street. 1890s. An American Main Street much as it looked in the last decade of the 19th century. The false fronts extending over the second stories are exaggerated, presumably lending prestige to the commercial property. A high proportion of the facade is window, typical of Victorian architecture, but here brought to a higher level with outsized bay windows in addition to street level windows for the display of goods.

ABOVE: 435 North Main Street. Built circa 1889. Original home of the *Fort Bragg Advocate-News,* founded 1889. The 1906 earthquake moved the huge rotary press several inches but the building had only slight damage.

MIDDLE RIGHT: 536 Oak Street.

BOTTOM RIGHT: 418 Main Street. Built 1896. One of Fort Bragg's earliest hospitals.

TOP: 460 North Franklin Street. Italianate cottage. Every part of this Italianate style house is scaled down. It has the cube shape and shallow roof of an Italianate with ornamental roof brackets, where little support is required. Similarly, the trim around the window is "heavy" for the scale of the house.

BELOW: 660 Harrison Street. Queen Anne. The decorative gingerbread on the house may be only a remnant of past glories. Compared to the Italianate cottage above, this houses stretches out like a cat luxuriating in the sunlight, with long horizontal lines marking every level.

FORTUNA

After being called both Slide and Springfield, Fortuna became the official name of this town in the late 1880s. The town's location among the Redwood forest, the Pacific Ocean, and the lush Eel River Valley contributed to its prosperity and growth. In 1891, a railroad depot was built on the line connecting San Francisco and Eureka, giving Fortuna and the outside world opportunity to know each other.

Victorian architecture rose to a high level of popularity in late 19th century America when "just plain" folks could afford these charming homes. The railroads contributed to this trend. Decorative architectural trim could be mass-produced and sent to remote corners of the continent. By the same means, smaller towns could obtain sophisticated woodworking machinery. A crate of scrolled brackets could find its way to Fortuna where carpenters employed the pieces according to personal taste. Instead of the high-style Victorians of San Francisco, we speak now of Folk Victorian. With all their trim and spindles, these houses suggest Queen Annes, but unlike Queen Annes, these are orderly, symmetrical houses. They do not have towers or elaborate moldings. Behind a Folk Victorian is a simple house: solid, practical, and enduring.

While some locales such as San Francisco or Ferndale have pronounced historical awareness, such awareness is yet to be matched in Fortuna. Nevertheless, Fortuna has a wealth of beautiful Victorians, large and small.

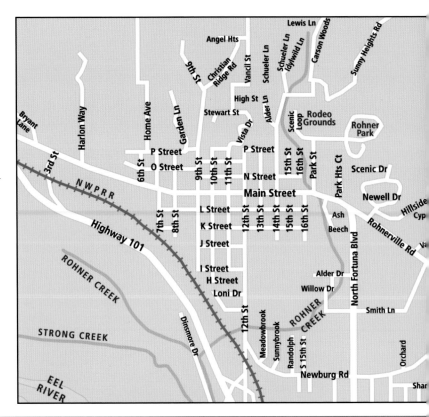

510 15th Street. Queen Anne cottage. Basking in the morning sun, this house makes an inviting sight with its handsome and neat trim. The rose garden's arbor with benches invite the visitor to rest.

ABOVE: 814 O Street. Stick. A grand, complex Victorian layout. The deep eaves with their decorative trusses are outstanding. The white trim emphasizing verticality, the wooden wall surfaces, the steeply pitched roof are all according to Stick ideals.

BELOW: 9th Street. The Grace Chapel. Victorian style church. This roof design is evocative of several styles: at once Gothic and Tyrolean. The central spire is so complete unto itself as to suggest an independent edifice sitting amongst and towering over the roofs of other buildings.

TOP: 884 8th Street. Queen Anne cottage. This house appears to be much smaller from the front than it actually is. This house is quite large from front to rear.
BELOW: 812 O Street. Stick. It may be of interest to compare this house with the large grey and white Stick at 814 O Street (shown on page 23, top) which sits next door. The two houses are actually very similar. But, the painting of this house de-emphasizes the very Stick features which are so prominent on its neighbor. Here it is the horizontal lines of the porch and the roof which seem to stand out.

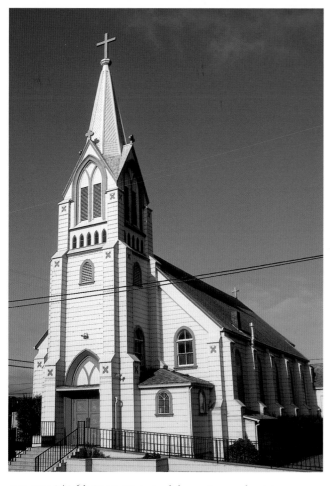

TOP LEFT: 945 6th Street. Restrained decorations and quiet coloration enhance this Folk Victorian.

TOP RIGHT: 968 9th Street. Folk Victorian. The yellow paneled door with its diminutive porch with outsize gingerbread make a charming Victorian statement.

ABOVE: 14th Street at N Street. St. Joseph's Catholic Church. Victorian Church with Eastlake touches embellishing the distinguished and well-proportioned spire.

MIDDLE RIGHT: 856 8th Street. Folk Victorian. This house is very similar in concept to the house shown above. A successful contractor or builder in an area would be able to resell his experience and this would result in such local similarities.

BOTTOM RIGHT: 136 Main Street. Italianate influence.

FERNDALE

A stroll in Ferndale is a trip back in time. The entire town has been designated a California State Historical Landmark. Nestled in the coastal hills and flanked by the Eel River, the rich land around Ferndale has supported a thriving dairy industry since the late 1800s. Seth and Stephen Shaw explored the area in 1852. Noting the luxuriously growing ferns, Seth Shaw gave the name Fern Dale to the area's first house which he built.

By 1878, a census of the surrounding area showed a population of about 1,400, a count which did not include members of the Wiyot tribe who also lived here. During this period Humboldt County was sparsely populated, giving ample opportunity for hard-working immigrants. Ferndale became a melting pot of Swiss-Italian, Scandinavian, and later, Portuguese cultures. The ornate homes built by successful dairy farmers became known as *Butterfat Palaces* and Ferndale acquired the nickname *Cream City.*

In the 20th century, logging was carried out with ignorant disregard for its effect on the ecosystem. In 1955 a disastrous flood hit Ferndale. The farmers and dairymen were just recovering when an even worse flood hit in 1964. Ferndale itself was spared but almost became a ghost town. Luckily Ferndale did recover.

In the 1940s there was talk of razing the old buildings on Main Street. But, there came about a fortunate development: Second-generation Ferndale resident Viola McBride joined forces with the town's newspaper and bought any building that was threatened with demolition. The publisher of the *Enterprise* persuaded locals to paint Main Street. Color consultants arrived and in a single weekend Ferndale's residents turned magnificent Victorians into dazzling showcases. The fever spread as residents splashed every imaginable color on the Victorians facing Ferndale's side streets. With this burst of color, Ferndale's fame grew.

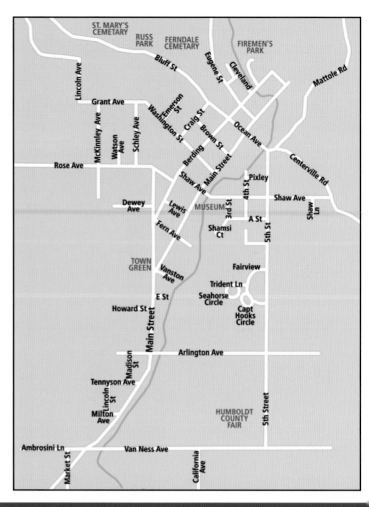

703 Main Street. **The Shaw House.** Gothic Revival with steeply pitched roof and decorative sawn details. Ferndale's oldest home. Seth Louis Shaw, the founder of Ferndale built his 14 room home between 1854 and 1856. The house has over an acre of gardens and trees on Francis Creek. It is now the Shaw House Inn.

ABOVE: 400 Berding Street. **The Dr. Hogan Ring Home and Hospital.** Queen Anne with Eastlake details. Built 1898. With an exquisite octagonal turret, carved details, gables, crested roof, and lush English landscaping, it is a masterpiece. For a time this building was abandoned and fell into a state of dilapidation. It was almost demolished. Fortunately it was bought in the 1960s and restored. It is now the Gingerbread Mansion B&B.

TOP: **400 Berding Street.**
Victorian interiors are elegantly and lavishly furnished with art, antiques, rich wall papers, and ornate furniture. In the ideal Victorian home every room gets the full treatment. Bathrooms are no exception . Ferndale's Bed and Breakfasts draw rave reviews for the innumerable touches of authentic Victoriana with which they have been graced.

OPPOSITE: 475 Main Street. Stick-Eastlake. Built 1898. Originally, this was the Red Star Clothing Company. Today the decorations have been painted for a highly expressive and artistic effect.

TOP: Main Street, Ferndale, U.S.A.

ABOVE: 290 Francis Street. Paint has enhanced the rhythmic detailing of the elaborate cornice and the windows of this Italianate.

ABOVE: 1042 Main Street. **The Dauphiny House.** Queen Anne-Eastlake. Built 1899. A classic Queen Anne bay window with colored glass panels. The frieze over the porch is especially handsome.

LEFT: 541 Berding Street. **The Neibur House.** Georgian-Stick. Built 1895. The Georgian influence is seen in the subdued use of decorative elements resulting in a more formal appearance and making the facade itself more prominent.

OPPOSITE TOP: 1249 Rose Avenue. **The Taubman House.** Stick/Eastlake with Queen Anne details. Built 1899 by architect and carpenter W. S. Fitzel for Taubman, owner of the Red Star Clothing Store.

OPPOSITE RIGHT: 831 Street. **The Hart Home.** Italianate. Built 1895. The turned veranda posts and sawn wood brackets on the porch create a rhythmic arch effect. Its cubic shape is enhanced by tall windows, a large cornice, large eaves brackets, quoins, and a low-pitched roof.

ABOVE AND LEFT: 455 Ocean Avenue. **The Arnold Berding Home.** Stylistically, a transitional design: the scrolled bargeboards are Carpenter Gothic; the bay window is Stick; and the pedimented windows and quoins are Italianate. Built in 1875 by the pioneer owner of the first general merchandise store in Ferndale. This house has been continuously occupied by the family for four generations. The coast cypress trees were planted in 1865 and have always been trimmed in their present shape. They are commonly referred to as Gumdrop trees.

OPPOSITE TOP: 835 Howard Street. Italianate, contrasting with most of the ornate Queen Annes and Stick styles of Ferndale. A widow's walk does the job of the more traditional cupola or belvedere.

OPPOSITE RIGHT: 923 Main Street. **The Smith House.** Built 1894. Queen Anne-Eastlake. Carved wood sunburst appliques decorate the Queen Anne roof gables while a collection of Eastlake details cover the building. Italianate quoins at the corners highlight the vertical lines.

EUREKA

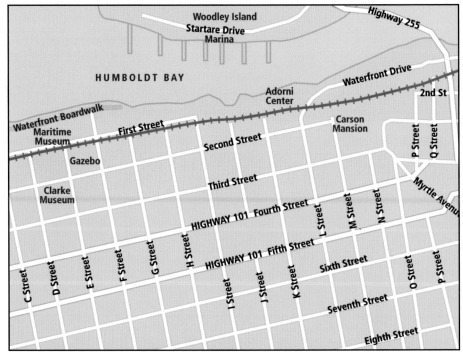

Eureka lies in the heart of the Redwood Empire, famous for the magnificent coastal giants, *Sequoia sempervirens.* They are the tallest trees in the world and played an important part in the development of Eureka's history. Its location on Humboldt Bay and the abundance of lumber provided a rich environment for the rise of this 19th century seaport. Miners, loggers, and fishermen came to settle this wilderness, and Eureka was founded in 1850.

Gold was discovered in the nearby Trinity area. By 1854, seven lumber mills were processing lumber and shipping it via 140 schooners out of Humboldt Bay to other booming cities along the coast. The bay was also host to a hugely successful fishing industry. Salmon fisheries already existed on the Eel River in 1851. Within seven years 2,000 barrels of cured fish and 50,000 pounds of smoked salmon were processed and shipped out of Humboldt Bay.

Eureka grew and prospered. Stately Victorians arose along the waterfront reflecting great prosperity. Many of them remain today in their original elegance and splendor.

ABOVE: 1025 J Street. Eastlake. Painted in soft and glowing colors, this modestly sized house has beautiful appliqued details. Unusual is the clock set below the eaves of the dormer.

OPPOSITE: 202 M Street (across the street from the Carson Mansion). **The Pink Lady.** Queen Anne. Designed by the Newsom brothers and built in 1889. It was a wedding gift from the lumber magnate William Carson to his son Milton and his new bride Mary Bell Carson. With a variety of shingle styles, an especially handsome Queen Anne window on the ground floor, the singular domed turret, and the wealth of decorative woodwork, it is an outstanding house. Its pink and white coloration do indeed bring to mind the term Wedding Cake architecture.

TRUMP &
SAUBLE INC.
ARCHITECTURE & PLANNING
202 M St. Eureka, CA 95501 (707) 443-2243

143 M Street. **The Carson Mansion.** Queen Anne with elements from every Victorian style. In fact, it brings to mind the extravagant castles of Ludwig of Bavaria built in the 1860s. It is just such homes that make the stuff of dream homes for children and adults alike. Designed by the Newsom brothers and built 1884–86. The house, sitting on a hill next to the bay and peering down Second Street, dominates the corner and the entire town as well. A tower soaring to 68 feet, intricate moldings, massive carved pillars with spindle work, stained glass windows, and copious gingerbread decorations: all that signifies Victorian. In building this house, lumber magnate William Carson employed the woodworkers from his mills during several depressed economic seasons to give them work and not lose these skilled workers. Surprisingly, the house only contains three bedrooms. Carson's children had grown up and moved out by the time it was built, so he felt no need for many more bedrooms. The Carson Mansion is a true masterpiece of Victorian architecture.

1033 3rd St. **The Carter House Inn.** A new-old Queen Anne. Built 1981. This building has an unusual story. Mark Carter, a native of Eureka, saw plans for the 1884 Murphy Mansion which stood in San Francisco until the 1906 earthquake. It had been designed by Samuel and Joseph Newsom, the architectural team responsible for the Carson Mansion. Carter decided to rebuild the Murphy Mansion on the corner lot diagonally across from the Hotel Carter in 1981. It now forms an enclave of four Victorian hotels in the heart of Old Town Eureka. In recent years the building has been painted this bright yellow which enhances the lively forms that are melded into this dynamic design. Considered together with the Carson Mansion, it is clear that the brothers Newsom had a distinct and elaborate style.

ABOVE: 1022, 1027, 1033 3rd Street. The Carter House Inn with it's two Victorian neighbors make a charming trio.

OPPOSITE: 1440 B Street

ABOVE : 2nd Street between E Street and F Street. Beautifully preserved and handsomely painted Victorian shops. Over a hundred years ago, these shops were all here when 2nd Street was the principal artery for the city. William Carson's house dominated the view at the end of Second Street as it does now. Carson had recognized the significance of this site.

LEFT : 216 F Street. A window set into the corner of the second floor creates this tiny balcony and an opportunity to turn on the Victorian spindle work charm. Sunlight finishes the job.

OPPOSITE TOP : 123 F Street, northwest corner of F and 2nd Streets. The style is known as Second Empire Commercial and is noted for its use of mansard roofs and Wedding Cake decorations. There is a layered look with different styles of columns on every floor. The ground floor corner has been remodeled and has lost its columns. The building occupies a very important place, facing the gazebo in the Old Town's square.

OPPOSITE BOTTOM: 117 F Street. **The Snug Building.** Eastlake. This handsomely-proportioned, commercial building has a falsely extended top, a feature seen often in such commercial properties. But an effort has been made to give the false front volume by the simple measure of adding a side piece. The result is quite effective.

1406 C Street. Eastlake. One of the prettiest entryways in Eureka. Eureka is unusual in the number of distinctly Eastlake houses it has. As a style, Eastlake has suffered because of the high level of maintenance work required to keep all the wood in good shape. As a result, many have been savagely modernized, or worse, demolished.

W hen in 1850, the Union Company laid out the town of Union (renamed Arcata in 1860), it had the foresight to designate a common plaza. For many of the hardy workers migrating to the area for the Trinity Mountain gold fields and nearby lumber camps, this town square was reminiscent of the New England towns they had come from. In those early days, arrivals camped in tents or huts in Arcata Plaza. Some even grazed their cows and goats there. Arcata grew predominantly as a lumber town and throughout much of this century was dotted with lumber mills.

Arcata makes extensive efforts to preserve, revitalize, and restore the architectural structures of the past and has an active program to protect the city's structures and features. The Clark Historical Museum has fine, well-preserved specimens of Victorian wardrobes, bureaus, desks, and clothes.

The City of Arcata is located in Humboldt County, on California's Redwood Coast, at the juncture of California Highway 101 and 299 West, also known as the Trinity Scenic Byway. Arcata is situated between three nationally known outdoor attractions: Redwood National Park, 35 miles to the north; Six Rivers National Forest, 40 miles to the east; and Avenue of the Giants, 60 miles to the south.

As in the rest of Humboldt County, Arcata has had a history of moderate but consistent growth. The 1990 census reported Arcata's population as 15,197 and the county population as 119,118. Arcata's weather is typical of the northern California coast, with mild summers and cool, moist winters.

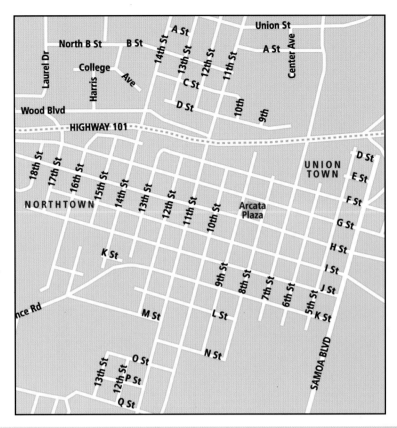

1022 Tenth Street. **The William Nixon House.** Carpenter's Gothic. Built in 1858 by a Dutch carpenter, who through local merchant Augustus Jacoby secured choice materials which had been shipped around Cape Horn. It became the property of Jacoby and stood vacant until 1861 when William Nixon bought it for 500 sacks of potatoes worth about $1,000. The Nixon family occupied the house for more than a century. A very fine carved bargeboard edges the front gable. The balustrade on the second floor echoes the pattern of the leaded panes in the casement windows. It is one of Arcata's earliest homes.

TOP: 860 10th Street. Built 1876. Queen Anne. The house was remodeled in 1902. The conical roofs of the rounded tower and turret are trimmed with ornamental fish-scale shingles, as is the second floor. Tiny dentil trim is used extensively. The windows are dramatized with borders of small panes in geometric patterns. The second story arched windows have unusual cornices. Both turret and tower have carved glass.

ABOVE: 986 12th Street. Queen Anne. Built in 1900 by local mill manager Frank Jacobs. Notice the letter "J" in the elaborate bas relief over the porch. Particularly graceful carved bargeboards on the two roof gables, diamond-shaped shingles, a lovely Queen Anne window on the second floor, and cut-out work under the porch gable, all add up to a harmonious Queen Anne unity.

ABOVE AND RIGHT: **Mirror Image Mansions.** Both Queen Anne with Italianate windows.

TOP: 902 14th Street . **The Stone House.** Built by Arcata's first banker, W.W. Stone

RIGHT: 980 14th Street. **The Jackson House.** Built by Elisha Jackson, a lumberman from Maine. In 1886, Arcata opened its first bank, the Bank of Arcata. It was at this period that the twin mansions were built. Homes of this period were centers for family and social activities. They were status symbols and decorated accordingly. Atop the turret of these two homes are handsome finials. Each boasted a third floor ballroom, each with the then-fashionable palladian window, an arched center unit flanked by rectangular sections. An Etruscan key design under the eaves borders each house.

TOP LEFT: Corner of 11th Street and J Street. **Pythian Castle.** The Knights of Pythias erected this unusual and imposing castle in 1885 at a time when lodges and churches substantially filled the need for social activities outside the home.

TOP RIGHT: 1651 J Street. Queen Anne.

ABOVE AND MIDDLE RIGHT: 916 13th Street. **The Bair House.** Queen Anne. Built in 1888 by Dr. Bangs, but lived in for 40 years by the Bair family. Tom Bair started in life as an orphan but rose to become an astute businessman who amassed a fortune. This is the most elaborate home in Arcata. The outstanding features include the lacy key-hole entrance arch, the round group of windows on the second floor, and the skirted turrets with carved panels and topped by witch's hats. There is an elegant carriage house at the rear.

BOTTOM RIGHT: 980 13 Street. **Dr. Horel's Sanitarium.** Built 1893, remodeled in 1904, it is another of Arcata's fine towers. Carved filigree fills the gable which faces J Street. Delicately patterned bargeboards outline the gable next to the tower.

A crescent-shaped beach which defines its harbor gives the city its name. In this area, the shore line looks much as it did 400 years ago, with longs stretches of untarnished beaches. Treasure seekers discovered the beautiful bay and laid out a city there less than a year later. Highway 101 passes through the city on the way to the Oregon Coast. Highway 199 follows the Smith River inland toward Oregon's Illinois Valley and the southern interior.

Crescent City has an interesting history museum and makes a good base for exploring Redwood National Park and the Smith River, one of the great recreational rivers in the world.

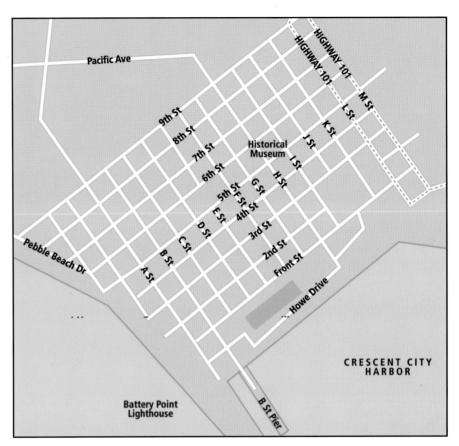

BELOW: 110 3rd Street at A Street. Folk Queen Anne-Carpenters Gothic. Without the complex plan of a grand Victorian, the house nevertheless achieves a feeling of Victorian drama with the placement of the large-scale pointed dormer. The cut-out arches with shamrocks on the porch and the diamond lattice under the gable eaves are perfectly proportioned to carry through this feeling.

TOP LEFT: 376 4th at D Street. An interesting use of curving arches set into outer pointed arches fulfills the Victorian love for complex roof lines.

TOP RIGHT: 622 J Street. Queen Anne. As with many Victorians, the porch is a very important element. Here spindle columns, a pedimented roof, and fancy brackets do the job. Another interesting embellishment is found in the semi-circular lines on the top dormer.

ABOVE: 680 J Street. Queen Anne. The arched-panel windows are carried through on both floors. The curved roof dormer adds a touch of oriental exoticism to this classically asymmetrical Victorian.

508 H Street. **The Eldredge House.** Built circa 1879. However sober-minded this Victorian may be, it possesses a very fine stately presence and a clear sense of proportion.

710 H Street at 7th Street. **The McNulty House.** Built 1897. Queen Anne. A supremely Victorian roof line graces this handsome house, combining a large-scale dormer with a pyramidal main roof. The present color combination of the house takes full advantage of the spirited decorative elements. The dormered bay window fulfills the Victorian ideal of asymmetrical unity.

Victorian Styles

THE VICTORIAN PERIOD Queen Victoria ruled in England from 1837 to 1901. The **Victorian Style** chiefly relates to the period 1880–1910.

QUEEN ANNE 1880–1910. Took hold in the Eastern U.S. in 1876 and spread to the West by the 1880s. It draws from all the other Victorian styles and is the most elaborate Victorian style. Often built with projecting gables, a round or octagonal tower at the corner with a onion or witch's hat shaped roof. Siding is often a mix of shingles of different patterns used to delineate stories of the house. Windows may be Palladian or composite forms. Elaborate, carved spindle work is common on the front porch.

CARPENTER GOTHIC A style of the 1850s characterized by a steeply pitched roof, decorative sawn details, lacy patterned bargeboards.

GOTHIC REVIVAL The first of the Victorian Styles. In the West 1850–70. Very few of these remain in Northern California. The style is very picturesque with steeply-pitched roofs with ornate bargeboards. Many have pointed arched windows. Either the upper panes are cut to that shape or the trim around the window makes it appear to be pointed.

ITALIANATE In the West 1860–85. Inspired by British models which in turn were based on romanticized Italian farmhouses and villas. These houses will have stylistic references to classical design. Generally, there will be full or half columns to the sides of the windows which will be tall and narrow, often rounded at the top. Bay windows are angled. Roofs are low-pitched and often hipped. Ornamentation, such as quoins, are either made of stone or made to look like stone. Eaves will have heavy brackets. Porch canopies often have heavy supporting brackets.

STICK OR EASTLAKE 1870–85. In the West these Stick and Eastlake styles were intermingled. The style is not classical, nor was it a revival style. It can be said to be an American style. In its heyday, it was considered very modern. Pieces of wood, the so-called sticks, are used as decoration. Brackets are curved with knobs, spindles, and other conventions used in furniture decoration. Very often there are small, rectangular incised or carved panels under windows and eaves, massive turned porch posts, cutout friezes.

Glossary of Terms

APPLIQUE Decoration, usually carved wood, attached to the surface.

BARGEBOARD A projecting board attached to the edge of a roof gable, often carved.

bargeboard

BAY WINDOW A large window or series of windows projecting from the outer wall of a building and forming a nook within.

BRACKET A structure in the shape of an L. Decorative or weight-bearing, supporting roofs, windows, etc.

CLAPBOARD SIDING Wood strips set horizontally over each other to create a weather-tight facing.

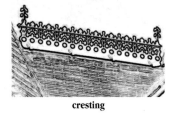
cresting

CORNICE A horizontal molded projection that crowns or completes a building or wall.

CRESTING Wood, or more commonly cast iron ornaments along the ridge of the roof or sometimes along the edge of the roof.

frieze

CUPOLA A small, domed and rounded roof tower with louvered or windowed sides.

EAVES The projecting overhang at the lower edge of a roof.

gambrel roof

FRIEZE A horizontal strip running between a cornice and architrave, can be plain or decorated with sculpture, scrolls, etc.

pediment

GABLE Triangular section of wall at the end of a pitched roof, occupying the space between the two slopes of the roof.

GAMBREL ROOF A ridged roof with two slopes on each side, the lower slope having a steeper pitch.

GINGERBREAD Term used to describe the elaborated ornamental and complex shapes attached to Victorian houses.

quoins

MANSARD ROOF A roof having two slopes on all four sides, the lower slope almost vertical and the upper almost flat.

PEDIMENT A wide low-pitched gable surmounting the facade of a building in the Grecian style and widely used in architecture and decoration.

Queen Anne Window

QUOIN Rectangles of stone, wood, or brick used to decorate corners of buildings.

QUEEN ANNE WINDOW The upper sash containing panels of colored glass.

truss

SASH The framework that holds the glass in a window.

WITCH'S TOWER A tower with a roof shaped like a witch's hat.

TRUSS A bracket used for support.

TURRET A small ornamental tower.

witch's hat